D0349470

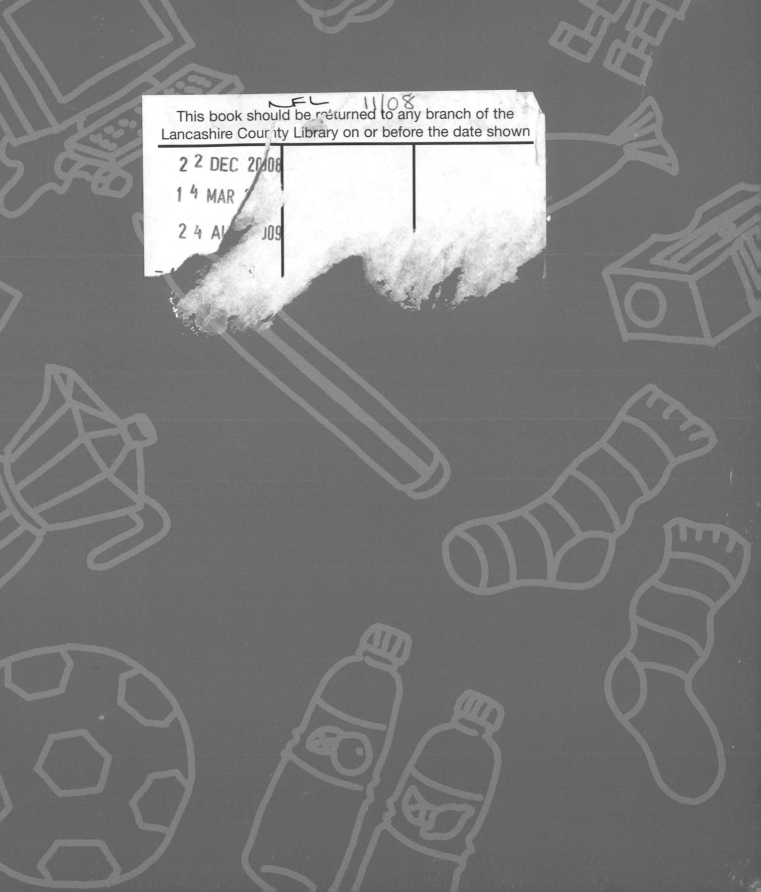

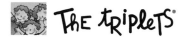

The Triplets

My First Picture
Dictionary

French-English

Illustrations: From the original drawings of Roser Capdevila
Text: Isabel Carril

CONTENTS

My First Picture
Dictionary

French-English

This picture dictionary introduces children to the marvellous world of words with colourful illustrations and simple translations.

Words are the key to a child's understanding of the world, and a sound acquisition of first words lays the foundations of successful language learning.

Learning is kept fun as children are guided through the pages of this picture dictionary by recurrent characters – young triplets. Children acquire new vocabulary and use their skills of observation, while they get to know the triplets' family, friends and school.

Parents can also suggest games to play, from searching for individual objects as well as the triplets in the larger illustrations, to answering the questions asked in the first and final pages of each chapter.

The games on the opening spread of each chapter are designed to introduce children to the chapter's theme. For example, in Family and friends, readers search the illustration for characters with particular attributes: tall, short, blond...

In the last spread of each chapter, words are introduced to explain how they are used to form sentences. For example, the final spread of Family and friends features words related to the expression "Who is it?" and "What are they doing?". Children can respond to these questions out loud, search for answers in the big illustrations throughout the chapter, and even use them to construct their own sentences.

Children will really enjoy expanding their vocabulary with this picture dictionary – and parents and teachers can join them in exploring the fascinating world of words.

La famille et les amis
Family and friends

Trouve quelqu'un de...
Find someone who is...

GRAND
TALL

PETIT
SHORT

GROS
STOUT

MINCE
THIN

Trouve quelqu'un avec...
Find someone who has...

LES CHEVEUX BLONDS
BLOND HAIR

LES CHEVEUX BRUNS
DARK HAIR

LES CHEVEUX LONGS
LONG HAIR

LES CHEVEUX COURTS
SHORT HAIR

LES CHEVEUX RAIDES
STRAIGHT HAIR

LES CHEVEUX FRISÉS
CURLY HAIR

Notre famille
Our family

GRAND-PÈRE
GRANDFATHER

GRAND-MÈRE
GRANDMOTHER

PÈRE
FATHER

MÈRE
MOTHER

FILS
SON

FILLE
DAUGHTER

FRÈRES
BROTHERS

SŒUR
SISTER

PETIT-FILS
GRANDSON

PETITE-FILLE
GRANDDAUGHTER

COUSIN
COUSIN

COUSINE
COUSIN

BÉBÉ
BABY

JUMELLES
TWINS

XYLOPHONE
XYLOPHONE

TAMBOURIN
TAMBOURINE

PIANO
PIANO

VIOLON
VIOLIN

TROMPETTE
TRUMPET

GUITARE
GUITAR

TAMBOUR
DRUM

AMPOULE
BULB

ENNUYEUX
BORED

DRÔLE
FUNNY

TRISTE
SAD

JOYEUX
HAPPY

FATIGUÉ
TIRED

CONFETTIS
CONFETTI

Nos amis
Our friends

PISCINE À BALLES
BALL POOL

QUILLES
SKITTLES

PETITS CHEVAUX
LUDO

PUZZLE
JIGSAW PUZZLE

MARIONNETTE
PUPPET

BOUGIES
CANDLES

TROTTINETTE
SCOOTER

PAIN AU LAIT
BUNS

JEU DE CUBES
BUILDING BLOCKS

CARTES
CARDS

CHÂTEAU
CASTLE

SKATEBOARD
SKATEBOARD

JEU ÉLECTRONIQUE
COMPUTER GAME

POUPÉES
DOLLS

BOISSONS
SOFT DRINKS

ROBOT
ROBOT

BALLON
BALLOON

TRICYCLE
TRICYCLE

AMIS
FRIENDS

DÉGUISEMENT
FANCY DRESS

NU-PIEDS
BAREFOOT

CHAUSSÉ
WEARING SHOES

BATEAU DE PIRATES
PIRATE SHIP

DRAPEAU
FLAG

GÂTEAU
CAKE

CUISINE DE JEU
TOY KITCHEN

PROPRE
CLEAN

SALE
DIRTY

La famille et les amis
Family and friends

ONCLE
UNCLE

TANTE
AUNT

NEVEU
NEPHEW

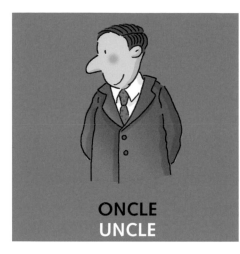

NIÈCE
NIECE

EMBRASSER
TO KISS

LIRE
TO READ

PARLER
TO TALK

CRIER
TO SHOUT

PRENDRE PAR LE BRAS
TO HUG

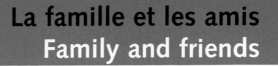

Qui est-ce?
Who is it?

Que font-ils?
What do they do?

CARESSER
TO CARESS

APPLAUDIR
TO APPLAUD

DANSER
TO DANCE

SOUFFLER
TO BLOW

TOMBER
TO FALL

ATTACHER
TO TIE

BAILLER
TO YAWN

CHANTER
TO SING

ÉCOUTER
TO LISTEN

La maison
The house

Où se trouve chaque dessin?
Where is each picture?

Est-il à droite ou à gauche des triplées?
Is it to the right or to the left of the triplets?

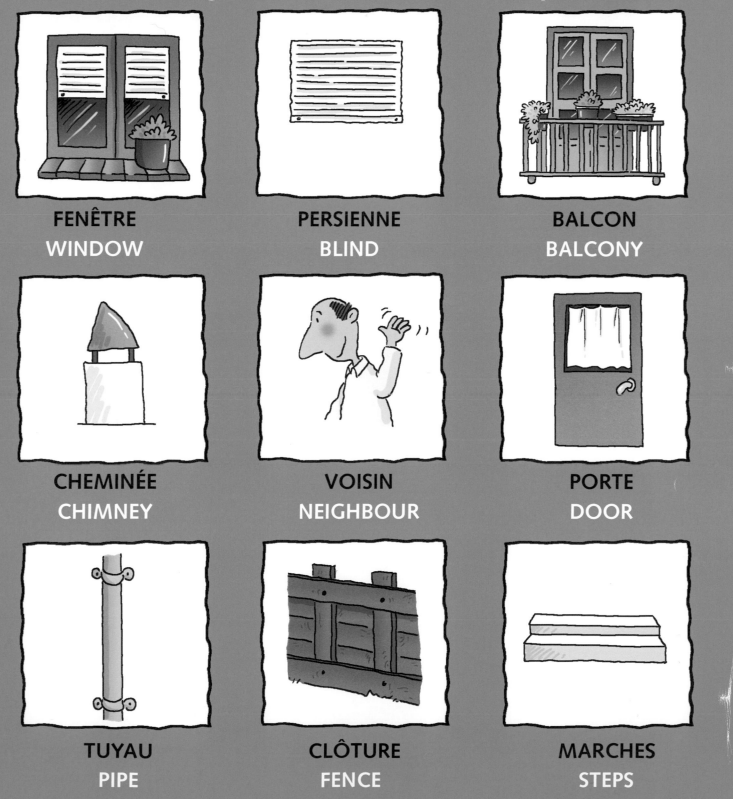

FENÊTRE	**PERSIENNE**	**BALCON**
WINDOW	BLIND	BALCONY
CHEMINÉE	**VOISIN**	**PORTE**
CHIMNEY	NEIGHBOUR	DOOR
TUYAU	**CLÔTURE**	**MARCHES**
PIPE	FENCE	STEPS

Notre salon-salle à manger
Our dining-living room

RIDEAU
CURTAIN

LIVRE
BOOK

LAMPE
LAMP

NAPPE
TABLECLOTH

SERVIETTE
NAPKIN

VERRE
GLASS

ÉTAGÈRES
BOOKSHELF

VASE
VASE

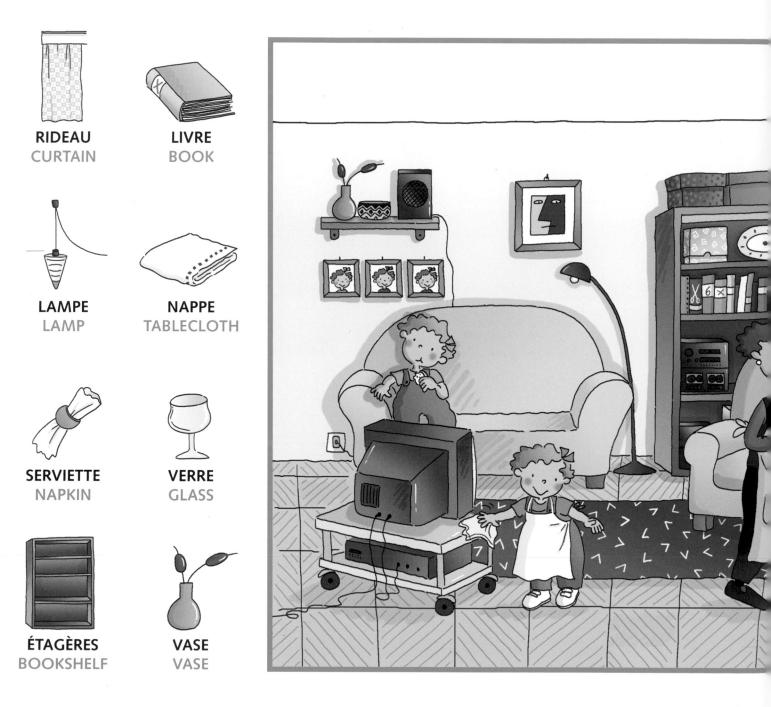

FAUTEUIL
ARMCHAIR

LECTEUR DVD
DVD

RIDEAU
NET CURTAIN

TABLEAU
PICTURE

TÉLÉVISION
TELEVISION

CANAPÉ
SOFA

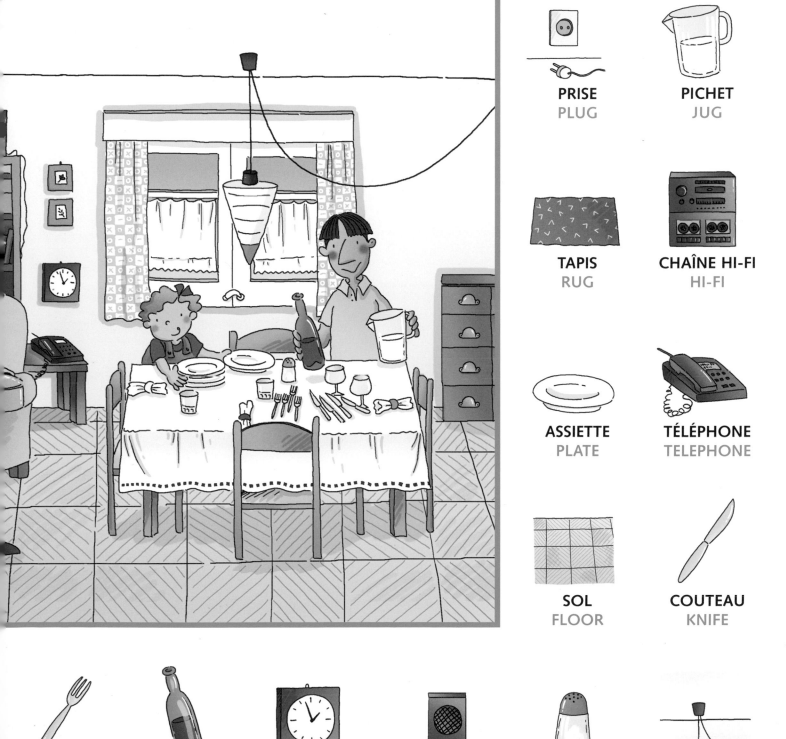

PRISE
PLUG

PICHET
JUG

TAPIS
RUG

CHAÎNE HI-FI
HI-FI

ASSIETTE
PLATE

TÉLÉPHONE
TELEPHONE

SOL
FLOOR

COUTEAU
KNIFE

FOURCHETTE
FORK

BOUTEILLE
BOTTLE

PENDULE
CLOCK

HAUT-PARLEUR
SPEAKER

SALIÈRE
SALTCELLAR

PLAFOND
CEILING

Notre chambre à coucher
Our bedroom

JUPE
SKIRT

CULOTTE
KNICKERS

ÉDREDON
EIDERDOWN

TIROIR
DRAWER

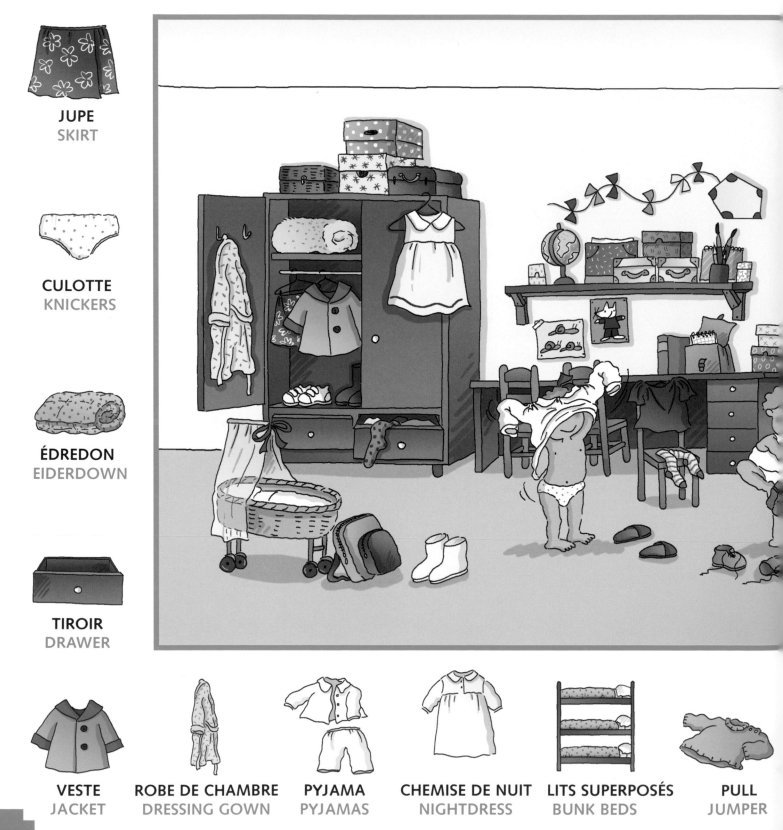

VESTE
JACKET

ROBE DE CHAMBRE
DRESSING GOWN

PYJAMA
PYJAMAS

CHEMISE DE NUIT
NIGHTDRESS

LITS SUPERPOSÉS
BUNK BEDS

PULL
JUMPER

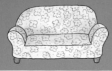
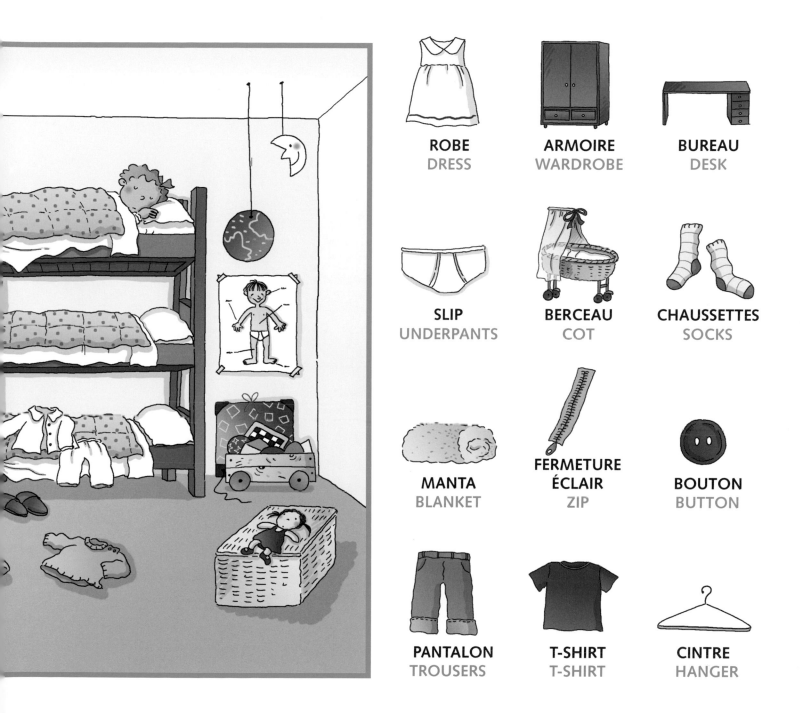

ROBE
DRESS

ARMOIRE
WARDROBE

BUREAU
DESK

SLIP
UNDERPANTS

BERCEAU
COT

CHAUSSETTES
SOCKS

MANTA
BLANKET

FERMETURE ÉCLAIR
ZIP

BOUTON
BUTTON

PANTALON
TROUSERS

T-SHIRT
T-SHIRT

CINTRE
HANGER

BOTTES
BOOTS

BASKETS
TRAINERS

CHAUSSONS
SLIPPERS

CHAUSSURES
SHOES

DRAP
SHEET

OREILLER
PILLOW

Notre cuisine
Our kitchen

CUISINIÈRE
COOKER

PLATEAU
TRAY

POÊLE
FRYING PAN

RÉFRIGÉRATEUR
FRIDGE

VIANDE
MEAT

POISSON
FISH

FRUITS
FRUIT

PASSOIRE
COLANDER

SUCRIER
SUGAR BOWL

YAOURT
YOGURT

FOUR
OVEN

MICRO-ONDES
MICROWAVE

POUBELLE
RUBBISH BIN

CAFETIÈRE
COFFEE POT

MARMITE
POT

BALAI
BRUSH

ÉVIER
SINK

ROBINET
TAP

LAVE-VAISSELLE
DISHWASHER

CONGÉLATEUR
FREEZER

MACHINE À LAVER
WASHING MACHINE

LÉGUMES
VEGETABLES

LAIT
MILK

CÉRÉALES
CEREAL

CHOCOLAT
CHOCOLATE

PAIN
BREAD

BISCUIT
BISCUIT

JUS DE FRUIT
JUICE

Notre salle de bains
Our bathroom

BRAS
ARM

COUDE
ELBOW

MAIN
HAND

DOIGT
FINGER

GENOU
KNEE

ÉPAULE
SHOULDER

POITRINE
BREAST

DOS
BACK

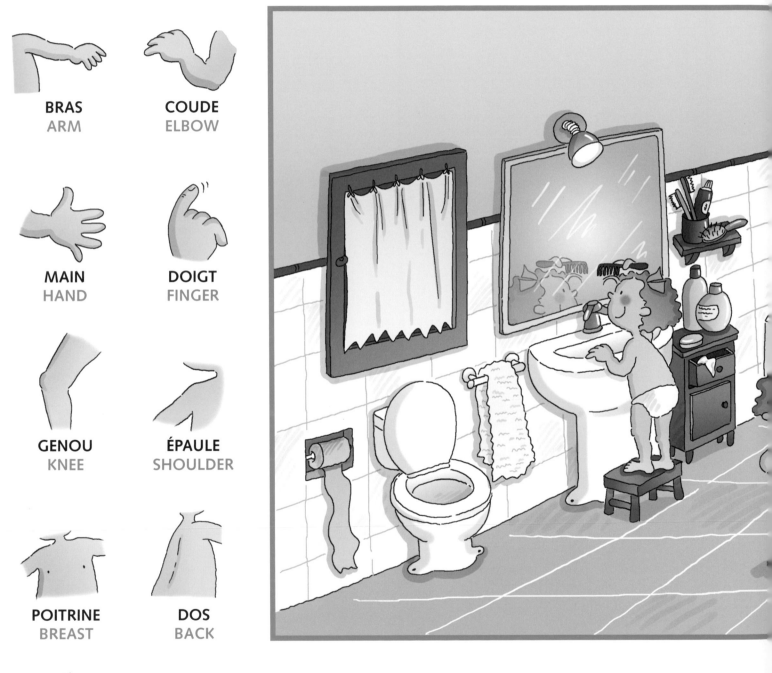

JAMBE
LEG

PIED
FOOT

CHEVILLE
ANKLE

FESSES
BOTTOM

FRONT
FOREHEAD

ŒIL
EYE

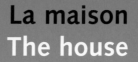

PAPIER TOILETTE
TOILET PAPER

DENTIFRICE
TOOTHPASTE

ÉPONGE
WASHBASIN

TOILETTE
TOILET

ESPONJA
SPONGE

JABÓN
SOAP

PORTE-SERVIETTES
TOWEL RACK

BAIGNOIR
BATH

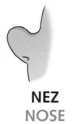
NEZ
NOSE

OREILLE
EAR

BOUCHE
MOUTH

DENTS
TEETH

LANGUE
TONGUE

COU
NECK

La maison
The house

PEIGNE
COMB

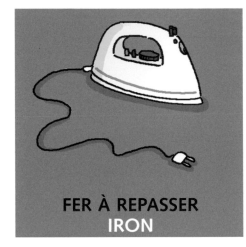

FER À REPASSER
IRON

DOUCHE
SHOWER

CUILLÈRE
SPOON

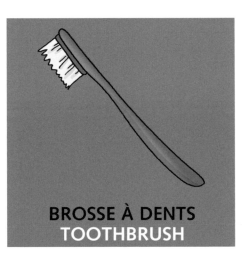

BROSSE À DENTS
TOOTHBRUSH

MIROIR
MIRROR

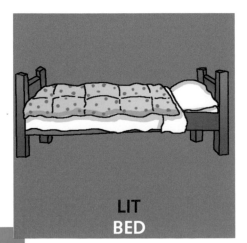

LIT
BED

VERRE
GLASS

CHIFFON
CLOTH

Qu'est-ce que c'est?
What is it?

A quoi est-ce que ça sert?
What is it used for?

SE PEIGNER
TO COMB

REPASSER
TO IRON

SE DOUCHER
TO TAKE A SHOWER

MANGER
TO EAT

SE LAVER LES DENTS
TO BRUSH YOUR TEETH

SE REGARDER
TO LOOK AT YOURSELF

DORMIR
TO SLEEP

BOIRE
TO DRINK

NETTOYER
TO CLEAN

L'école
The school

Je vois, je vois... une petite chose... De quelle couleur? Jaune! Qu'est-ce que c'est? Un poussin!

I spy, I spy... Something... What colour is it? Yellow! What is it? A chick!

JAUNE
YELLOW

BLEU
BLUE

ROUGE
RED

VERT
GREEN

ORANGE
ORANGE

MARRON
BROWN

VIOLET
PURPLE

BLANC
WHITE

NOIR
BLACK

Notre salle de classe
Our classroom

ORDINATEUR
COMPUTER

EFFACEUR
DUSTER

GOMME
ERASER

BURIN
BURIN

CRAIE
CHALK

TROUSSE
PENCIL CASE

CAGE
CAGE

FEUILLE DE PAPIER
SHEET OF PAPER

TUBE DE COLLE
GLUE STICK

TABLIER
BIB

STYLO
PEN

CHAISE
CHAIR

CRAYONS DE CIRE
WAX CRAYONS

HAMSTER
HAMSTER

CAHIER
NOTEBOOK

PEINTURE MURALE
MURAL

TABLE
TABLE

PINCEAU
PAINTBRUSH

TAILLE-CRAYONSS
PENCIL SHARPENER

POTS DE PEINTURE
PAINTS

AQUARIUM
FISHTANK

TABLEAU
BLACKBOARD

CRAYON
PENCIL

CHEMISE
FOLDER

PÂTE À MODELER
MODELLING PASTE

RÈGLE
RULER

CISEAUX
SCISSORS

ÉTAGÈRE
SHELF

Notre cour de récréation
Our playground

BALLON
BALL

SANDWICH
SANDWICH

FONTAINE
FOUNTAIN

BANC
BENCH

BALANÇOIRE
SWINGS

POTEAU DE BUT
GOALPOST

TOBOGGAN
SLIDE

TOUPIE
SPINNING TOP

SIFFLET
WHISTLE

BILLES
MARBLES

EAU
WATER

ARBRE
TREE

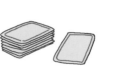

IMAGES
PICTURE CARDS

YOYO
YO-YO

AVION EN PAPIER
PAPER PLANE

SAC À DOS
BACKPACK

RATEAU
RAKE

FEUILLES
LEAVES

SABLE
SAND

CORDE À SAUTER
SKIPPING ROPE

GANTS
GLOVES

NŒUD
BOW

PELLE
SHOVEL

OISEAU
LITTLE BIRD

POT À FLEURS
FLOWERPOT

SEAU
BUCKET

CERCEAU
HOOPS

LUNETTES
GLASSES

L'école
The school

Qui sont-ils?
Who are they?

MAÎTRESSE
TEACHER

ARBITRE
REFEREE

GARDIENNE DE BUT
GOALKEEPER

SAUTER
TO JUMP

PLEURER
TO CRY

RIRE
TO LAUGH

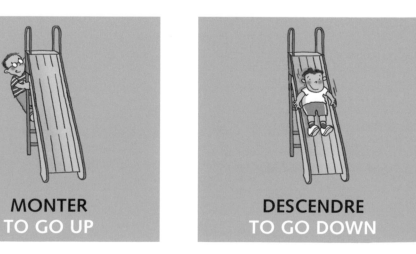

REBONDIR
TO BOUNCE

MONTER
TO GO UP

DESCENDRE
TO GO DOWN

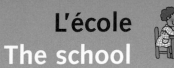
Que font-ils?
What do they do?

Comment vont-ils?
How are they?

Où est-ce que c'est?
Where is it?

JETER
TO THROW

COURIR
TO RUN

DEBOUT
STANDING

ASSIS
SITTING

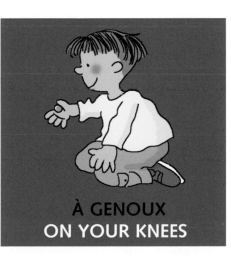

À GENOUX
ON YOUR KNEES

EN HAUT
UP

EN BAS
DOWN

DEDANS
INSIDE

DEHORS
OUTSIDE

La ville
The city

Cherche ces formes dans le dessin:
Find these shapes in the picture:

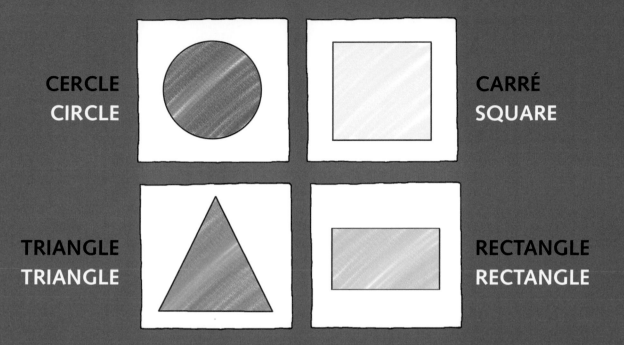

CERCLE
CIRCLE

CARRÉ
SQUARE

TRIANGLE
TRIANGLE

RECTANGLE
RECTANGLE

Quelle forme ont...?
What is the shape of a...?

TOIT
ROOF

ROUE
WHEEL

PANNEAU
SIGN

Cola

SAC
BAG

Notre rue
Our street

IMMEUBLE
BUILDING

BANQUE
BANK

PASSAGE POUR PIÉTONS
ZEBRA CROSSING

TROTTOIR
PAVEMENT

ROUTE
ROAD

GRATTE-CIEL
SKYSCRAPER

ARRÊT D'AUTOBUS
BUS STOP

MAGASIN
SHOP

ÉGLISE
CHURCH

CLOCHE
BELL

FEU DE CIRCULATION
TRAFFIC LIGHTS

LAMPADAIRE
STREET LAMP

STORE
AWNING

RESTAURANT
RESTAURANT

34

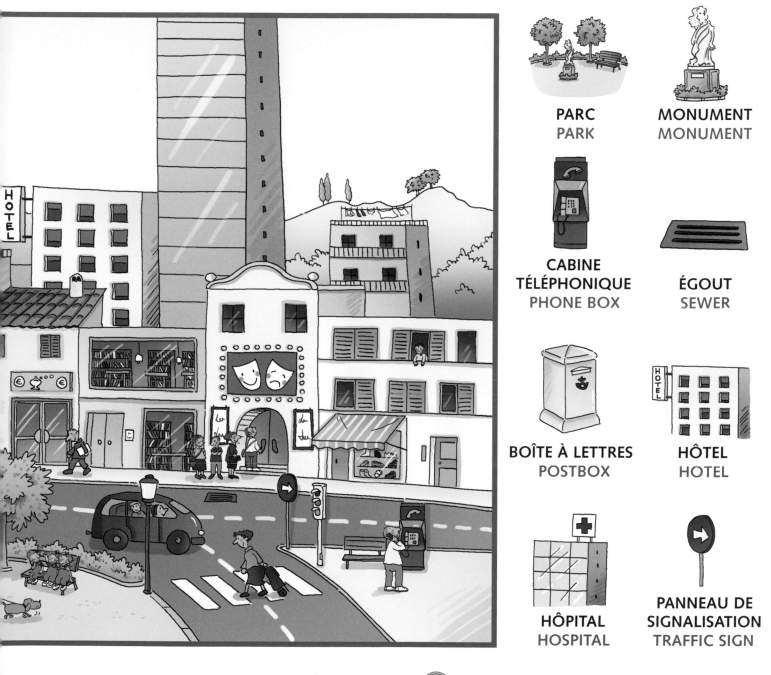

PARC
PARK

MONUMENT
MONUMENT

CABINE TÉLÉPHONIQUE
PHONE BOX

ÉGOUT
SEWER

BOÎTE À LETTRES
POSTBOX

HÔTEL
HOTEL

HÔPITAL
HOSPITAL

PANNEAU DE SIGNALISATION
TRAFFIC SIGN

CONDUCTEUR
DRIVER

PIÉTON
PEDESTRIAN

HÔTEL DE VILLE
TOWN HALL

THÉÂTRE
THEATRE

BIBLIOTHÈQUE
LIBRARY

CINÉMA
CINEMA

Le transport
The trip

VOITURE
CAR

MOTO
MOTORBIKE

**CAMION DE
POMPIERS**
FIRE ENGINE

VOLANT
STEERING
WHEEL

BICYCLETTE
BICYCLE

CASQUE
HELMET

GUIDON
HANDLEBARS

SELLE
SADDLE

PARKING
CAR PARK

VALISE
SUITCASE

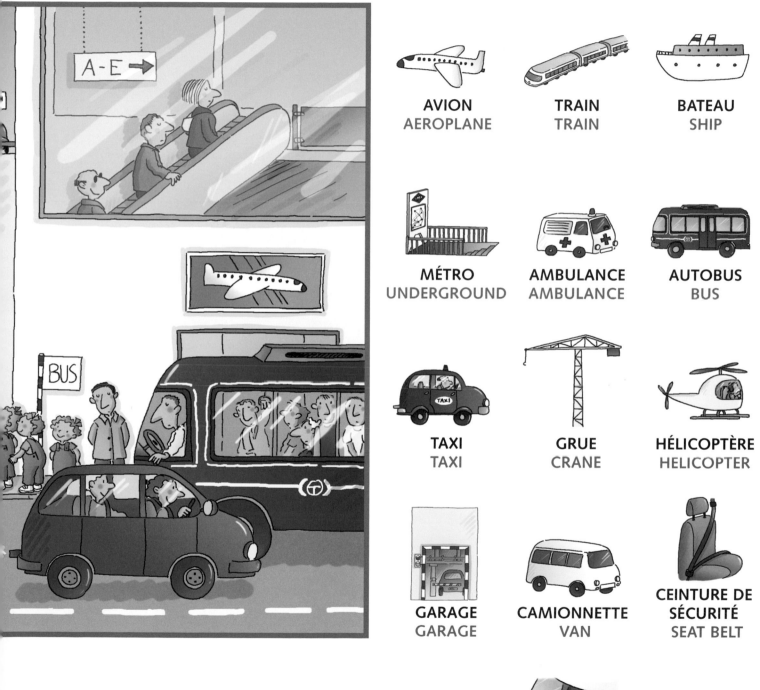

AVION
AEROPLANE

TRAIN
TRAIN

BATEAU
SHIP

MÉTRO
UNDERGROUND

AMBULANCE
AMBULANCE

AUTOBUS
BUS

TAXI
TAXI

GRUE
CRANE

HÉLICOPTÈRE
HELICOPTER

GARAGE
GARAGE

CAMIONNETTE
VAN

CEINTURE DE SÉCURITÉ
SEAT BELT

PÉDALE
PEDAL

WAGON
CARRIAGE

FENÊTRE
WINDOW

ROUTE
HIGHWAY

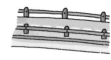

CONDUCTEUR DE TRAIN
TRAIN DRIVER

CAMION
LORRY

Que veux-tu être quand tu seras grand
What would you like to do when you

ARCHITECTE
ARCHITECT

ÉBOUEUR
REFUSE
COLLECTOR

CONCIERGE
CONCIERGE

FACTEUR
POSTWOMAN

INFORMATICIEN
IT SPECIALIST

DÉTECTIVE
DETECTIVE

PHARMACIENNE
PHARMACIST

COIFFEUSE
HAIRDRESSER

GARÇON DE CAFÉ
WAITER

COMMERÇANT
SHOPKEEPER

...w up?

PEINTRE
DÉCORATEUR
PAINTER

ÉCRIVAIN
WRITER

JARDINIÈRE
GARDENER

BALAYEUR
STREET
SWEEPER

DANSEUSE
DANCER

CUISINIÈRE
COOK

POLICIER
POLICEMAN

MÉCANICIEN
MECHANIC

PHOTOGRAPHE
PHOTOGRAPHER

INFIRMIÈRE
NURSE

MÉDECIN
DOCTOR

REPRESANTANT
SALESMAN

ACTRICE
ACTRESS

JOURNALISTE
JOURNALIST

MUSICIEN
MUSICIAN

SCIENTIFIQUE
SCIENTIST

CHANTEUSE
SINGER

CHAUFFEUR DE TAXI
TAXI DRIVER

Les sports
Sports

SAUT EN HAUTEUR
HIGH JUMP

SAUT EN LONGUEUR
LONG JUMP

COURSE DE HAIES
HURDLES

RUBAN DE GYMNASTIQUE
GYMNASTICS RIBBON

PATIN À GLACE
ICE SKATING

PATIN À ROULETTES
ROLLER SKATING

PANIER
BASKET

BONNET DE BAIN
SWIMMING CAP

BASKET
BASKETBALL

CLAQUETTES
FLIP-FLOPS

SURVÊTEMENT
TRACKSUIT

TAPIS
MAT

FOOTBALL
FOOTBALL

GYMNASTIQUE
GYMNASTICS

FAIRE GALIPETTE
SOMERSAULT

FAIRE LE POIRIER
HANDSTAND

GENOUILLÈRES
KNEE PADS

TENNIS
TENNIS

PATIN
ROLLER SKATE

BEACH VOLLEY
BEACH VOLLEYBALL

PING-PONG
PING-PONG

MAILLOT DE BAIN
SWIMSUIT

JUDO
JUDO

JOUEUR
PLAYER

JUSTAUCORPS
LEOTARD

NATATION
SWIMMING

FILET
NET

RAQUETTE
RACKET

La ville
The city

What do we do...

...dans la rue?

...in the street?

ATTENDRE L'AUTOBUS
TO WAIT FOR THE BUS

TÉLÉPHONER
TO MAKE A PHONE CALL

TRAVERSER
TO CROSS

CONDUIRE
TO DRIVE

STATIONNER
TO PARK

NAVIGUER
TO SAIL

PRENDRE LE TRAIN
TO GO BY TRAIN

FAIRE DU VÉLO
TO RIDE A BICYCLE

SIGNALER
TO POINT

...quand on voyage?

...when we travel?

...quand on fait du sport?

...when we play sports?

...quand on est grand?

...when we are adults?

MARQUER UN PANIER
TO SCORE

SE REPOSER
TO REST

SUER
TO SWEAT

SHOOTER
TO SHOOT

SIFFLER
TO BLOW A WHISTLE

TRAVAILLER
TO WORK

GUÉRIR
TO CURE

FAIRE DE LA RECHERCHE
TO INVESTIGATE

CUISINER
TO COOK

Les animaux et les plantes

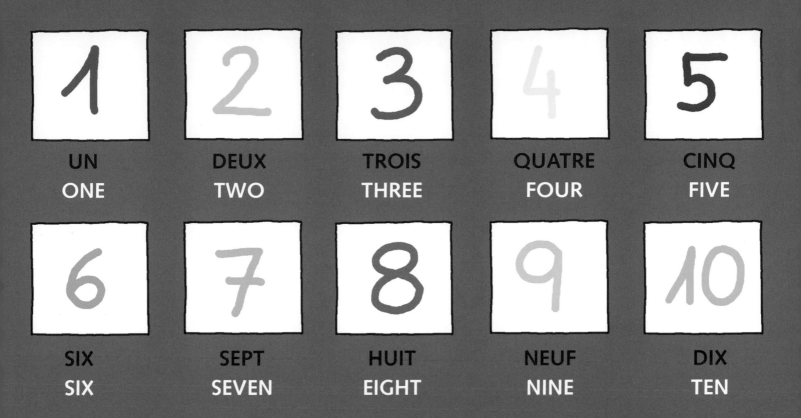

1	2	3	4	5
UN	DEUX	TROIS	QUATRE	CINQ
ONE	TWO	THREE	FOUR	FIVE

6	7	8	9	10
SIX	SEPT	HUIT	NEUF	DIX
SIX	SEVEN	EIGHT	NINE	TEN

Combien y-en-a-t'il?
How many are there?

ÉCUREUIL	SOURIS	LÉZARD	PAPILLON	COCCINELLE
SQUIRREL	MOUSE	LIZARD	BUTTERFLY	LADYBIRD

PIN	ROSE	TULIPE	MARGUERITE	LILAS
PINE	ROSE	TULIP	DAISY	LILAC

45

On va à la ferme
Let's go to the farm

POULE
HEN

CHEVAL
HORSE

CHÈVRE
GOAT

COQ
COCK

TRACTEUR
TRACTOR

ARROSOIR
WATERING CAN

HOUE
HOE

BROUETTE
WHEELBARROW

FERMIER
FARMER

MARE
POND

POUSSIN
CHICK

CANARD
DUCK

COCHON
PIG

ÂNE
DONKEY

LAPIN
RABBIT

BREBIS
SHEEP

VACHE
COW

GRENOUILLE
FROG

DIND
TURKEY

CHAT
CAT

AGNEAU
LAMB

**CHAMP
CULTIVÉ**
PLOUGHED
FIELD

GRANGE À FOIN
HAYLOFT

POTAGER
VEGETABLE GARDEN

OIE
GOOSE

PORCHERIE
PIGSTY

BASSE-COUR
FARMYARD

ÉCURIE
STABLE

On va au zoo
Let's go to the zoo

LION
LION

LÉOPARD
LEOPARD

OURS BRUN
BROWN BEAR

OURS POLAIRE
POLAR BEAR

PANTHÈRE
PANTHER

TIGRE
TIGER

RENNE
REINDEER

ÉLÉPHANT
ELEPHANT

RHINOCÉROS
RHINO

GORILLE
GORILLA

HIPPOPOTAME
HIPPO

ZÈBRE
ZEBRA

GIRAFE
GIRAFFE

PANDA
PANDA BEAR

KOALA
KOALA

SINGE
MONKEY

AIGLE
EAGLE

VAUTOUR
VULTURE

NID
NEST

CIGOGNE
STORK

HIBOU
OWL

PERROQUET
PARROT

KANGOUROU
KANGAROO

PINGOUIN
PENGUIN

CHAMEAU
CAMEL

SERPENT
SNAKE

PIGEON
PIGEON

MOINEAU
SPARROW

On va à l'aquarium
Let's go to the aquarium

REQUIN
SHARK

MORAINE
MORAY

RAIE
RAYFISH

POISSON CLOWN
CLOWNFISH

TORTUE
TORTOISE

ÉTOILE DE MER
STARFISH

OURSIN
SEA URCHIN

CALMAR
SQUID

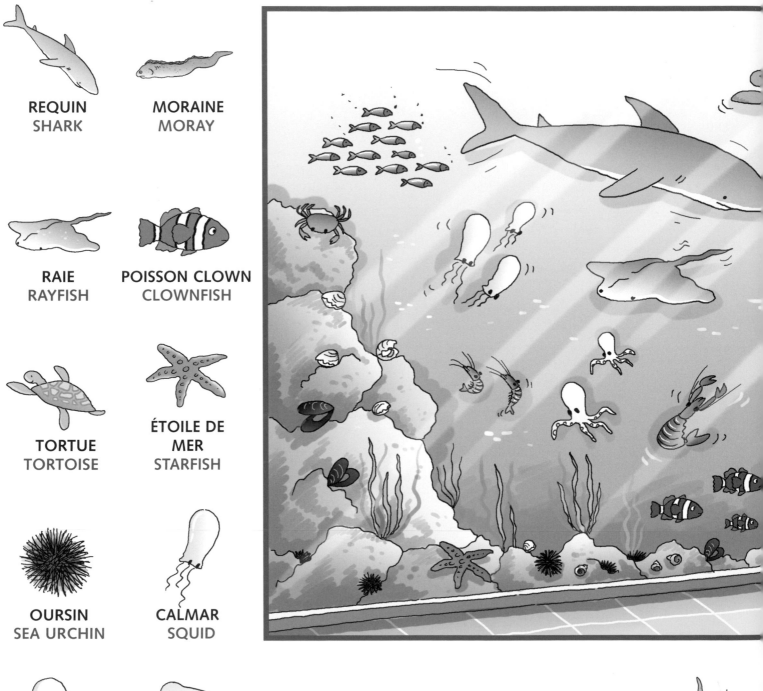

PIEUVRE
OCTOPUS

MÉDUSE
JELLYFISH

MOULE
MUSSEL

MERLU
HAKE

SOLE
SOLE

ALGUE
SEA WEED

CRABE
CRAB

SARDINE
SARDINE

HOMARD
LOBSTER

PALOURDE
CLAM

MORUE
COD

BIGORNEAU
WINKLE

CREVETTE ROSE
PRAWN

BERNICLE
LIMPET

OTARIE
SEAL

ORQUE
KILLER WHALE

DAUPHIN
DOLPHIN

OTARIE
SEAL

BALEINE
WHALE

MORSE
WALRUS

Les animaux et les plantes
Animals and plants

HOMME
MAN

FEMME
WOMAN

CHIEN
DOG

POISSON
FISH

SE PENCHER
TO LEAN OUT

SEMER
TO SOW

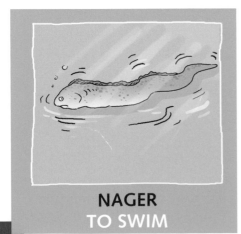

NAGER
TO SWIM

ENTRER
TO GO IN

SORTIR
TO GO OUT

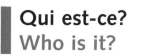

Qui est-ce?
Who is it?

Quel animal est-ce?
What animal is it?

Que font-ils?
What do they do?

OUVRIR
TO OPEN

FERMER
TO CLOSE

NOURRIR
TO FEED

VOLER
TO FLY

SALUER
TO SAY HELLO

ABOYER
TO BARK

MORDRE
TO BITE

GRIMPER
TO CLIMB

SE PROMENER
TO TAKE A STROLL

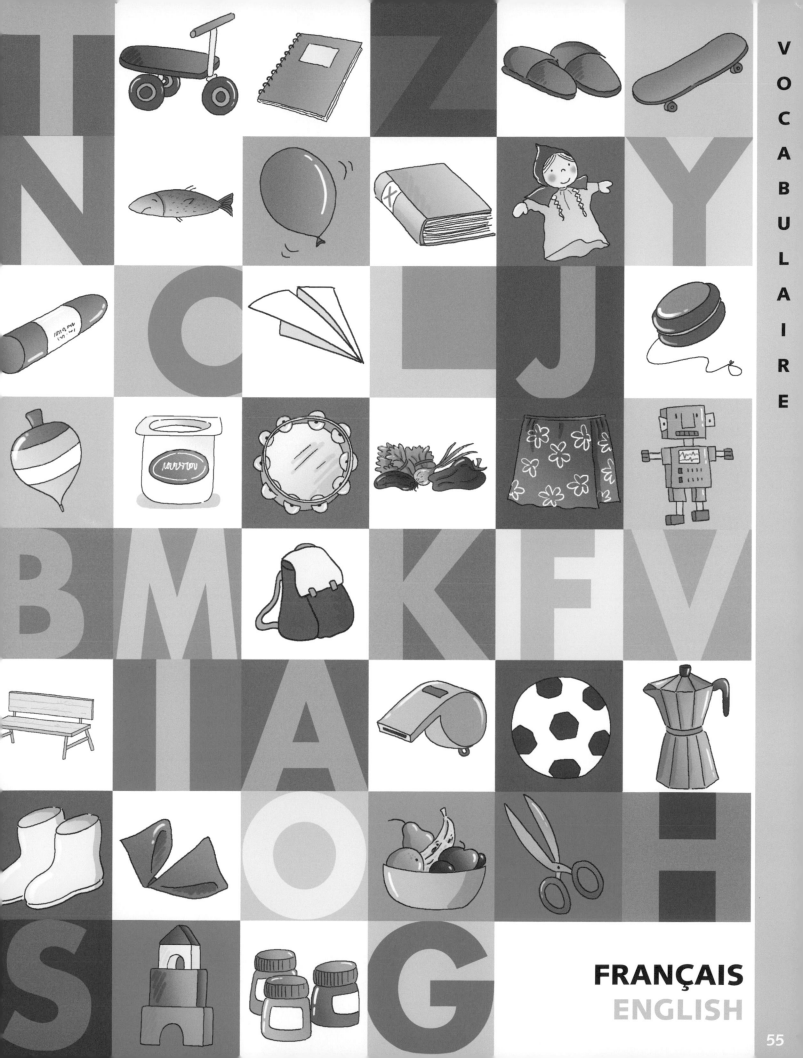

FRANÇAIS
ENGLISH

A
B
C
D
E
F
G
H
I
J
K
L
M
N
Ñ
O
P
Q
R
S
T
U
V
W
X
Y
Z

A
B
C
D
E
F
G
H
I
J
K
L
M
N
Ñ
o
P
Q
R
S
T
U
V
W
X
Y
Z

58

A B C D E F G H I J K L M N Ñ O **P** **Q** **R** **S** **T** U **V** **W** **X** **Y** **Z**

A B C D E F G H I J K L M N Ñ O P Q R S T U V W X Y Z

A
B
C
D
E
F
G
H
I
J
K
L
M
N
Ñ
O
P
Q
R
S
T
U
V
W
X
Y
Z

A
B
C
D
E
F
G
H
I
J
K
L
M
N
Ñ
O
P
Q
R
S
T
U
V
W
X
Y
Z

First published in the UK in 2008 by Wayland

© Cromosoma, SA y Televisió de Catalunya, 2008
© Grupo Editorial Bruño, S.L., 2008

Wayland
338 Euston Road
London NW1 3BH

Wayland Australia
Level 17/207 Kent Street
Sydney NSW 2000

Illustrations: from the original drawings of Roser Capdevila
Text: Isabel Carril
Translation into English: John Liddy

ISBN 9780750256926
ISBN Cromosoma:978-84-92419-17-3

Wayland is a division of Hachette Children's Books,
an Hachette Livre UK company.